CW00494623

WISDOM WHISPERS

DAILY AFFIRMATIONS FOR A FULFILLING LIFE

BY VERONICA WILLIAMS

CONTENTS

COPYRIGHT © 2023 VERONICA WILLIAMS
All Rights Reserved.

INTRODUCTION

Hey there, beautiful souls! Welcome to "Wisdom Whispers: Daily Affirmations for a Fulfilling Life." I'm thrilled you've picked up this book, and I can't wait to embark on this journey of self-discovery and positivity with you.

Life can be a rollercoaster, can't it? We all experience those highs that make us feel on top of the world, and, of course, those lows that leave us wondering if we'll ever catch a break. But here's the secret sauce: the way we navigate these ups and downs largely depends on our mindset and the daily dialogues we have with ourselves.

That's where this book comes in—think of it as your daily dose of encouragement, your pocket-sized cheerleader, and your guide to cultivating a life that truly resonates with joy and fulfillment. We're diving into the magical realm of affirmations, those powerful phrases that have the potential to transform the way you think, feel, and live.

Setting the Stage

Let's start by unpacking the term "affirmations." These aren't just wishful thinking or repeating words mindlessly; they're the intentional and positive statements we tell ourselves to foster a mindset of growth, resilience, and self-love. Affirmations are like little love notes to ourselves, reminders that we are capable, deserving, and worthy of all the goodness life has to offer.

In the hustle and bustle of our daily lives, it's easy to get caught up in the whirlwind of negativity— whether it's self-doubt, external pressures, or just the general chaos of the world. But, my friend, this book is your sanctuary. It's a space where you can retreat daily to recalibrate your thoughts, shift your perspective, and infuse your day with positivity.

The Blueprint for Fulfillment

Now, you might be wondering, "Why daily affirmations, and how can they truly make a difference?" Well, that's precisely what we're here to explore together. Each chapter of "Wisdom Whispers" is crafted with love and intention, addressing different facets of your life where affirmations can work their magic.

From the moment you open your eyes in the morning to the time you lay your head down at night, we're going to weave affirmations into the fabric of your day. We'll tap into the power of positive thinking, set the stage for success, nurture self-love, cultivate gratitude, and embrace change and resilience. We're covering it all, my friend!

Your Daily Companion

Think of this book as your trusty companion, your go-to source for daily inspiration and guidance. Whether you're a seasoned affirmation enthusiast or a newcomer to the world of positive thinking, there's something here for everyone. Each chapter is designed to offer practical insights, real-life examples, and a treasure trove of affirmations tailored to the specific theme.

But here's the beautiful part—it's not just about reading these affirmations; it's about embodying them.

It's about making these positive statements an integral part of your mindset, allowing them to ripple through your thoughts, actions, and, ultimately, your life. And the best part? You can start right now, right where you are.

Let's Dive In!

So, are you ready to embark on this journey with me? Are you ready to sprinkle a bit of magic into your everyday existence? "Wisdom Whispers" is not just a book; it's an invitation to transform your life from the inside out, one affirmation at a time.

As we dive into the pages that follow, let your guard down, open your heart, and embrace the potential for positive change. Together, we'll navigate the twists and turns of life armed with the wisdom of affirmations, creating a life that's not just fulfilling but truly magical.

Get ready for a daily dose of inspiration, a sprinkle of positivity, and a whole lot of love. "Wisdom Whispers" is not just a book; it's a journey, and I'm honored to be your guide.

Here's to a life filled with wisdom, whispers of positivity, and the fulfillment you deserve. Let the adventure begin!

CHAPTER 1. THE POWER OF POSITIVE THINKING

Hey there, amazing soul! Welcome to the first chapter of "Wisdom Whispers: Daily Affirmations for a Fulfilling Life." I'm so excited that you've decided to embark on this journey of positivity and self-discovery with me. Get ready because we're about to dive headfirst into the magical realm of "The Power of Positive Thinking."

Unveiling the Magic

Ever heard the saying, "Your thoughts shape your reality"? Well, it's not just a catchy phrase; it's a profound truth. This chapter is all about unraveling the enchanting world of positive thinking and understanding how the thoughts we cultivate can have a transformative impact on our lives.

The Impact of Thoughts on Well-being

Let's start by acknowledging the incredible power our thoughts hold. Picture your mind as a lush garden, with each thought as a seed. The quality of those seeds determines the beauty and vibrancy of your mental landscape. Positive thoughts act as the sunlight and nourishment that allow your garden to flourish, while negative thoughts can act like weeds, hindering growth and stealing the spotlight.

Think about a time when you woke up on the right side of the bed, with a smile on your face and a skip in your step. Didn't the day seem to unfold in a more positive way? Now, contrast that with a day when negativity took the reins. See the difference? Our thoughts have the power to shape our experiences, influencing how we perceive and respond to the world around us.

Introduction to Positive Affirmations

Now, let's talk about a little tool that can amplify the magic of positive thinking: affirmations. Affirmations are like the champions of your thought world, the positive warriors that stand guard against negativity. They're intentional statements crafted to shift your mindset, challenge self-sabotaging beliefs, and cultivate a positive outlook.

Affirmations act as a daily dose of encouragement, a gentle reminder that you are capable, deserving, and worthy of all the goodness life has to offer. In this chapter, we'll explore how positive affirmations can become your secret weapon for building a more optimistic and fulfilling life.

Examples of Positive Affirmations

So, what do these affirmations look like? Well, they can be as unique as you are! Positive affirmations are personal, and the ones that resonate with you might not work for someone else. However, let's sprinkle a bit of inspiration with some examples to get those creative affirmation juices flowing:

1. *I am worthy of love and respect in all areas of my life.*
2. *Every challenge I face is an opportunity for growth and learning.*
3. *I trust in the process of life and let go of my need for control.*
4. *My mind is filled with positive and loving thoughts.*

5. *I am a magnet for miracles, and I attract only good into my life.*

Feel free to borrow these or tweak them to fit your unique journey. The key is to choose affirmations that resonate with you on a deep, soulful level.

Building a Foundation for Success

Now that we've dipped our toes into the world of positive thinking and affirmations, let's talk about building a solid foundation for success. You know, setting the stage for a day filled with joy, accomplishment, and positivity.

Setting Intentions for the Day

Ever notice how the first moments of your day can set the tone for everything that follows? It's like the opening scene of a movie—it gives you a glimpse of what's to come. That's why we're going to explore the power of setting intentions for the day.

Imagine waking up and, before the hustle and bustle takes over, taking a moment to set a positive intention for the day. It could be as simple as declaring, "Today, I choose joy," or "I am open to the possibilities that today brings." By setting a positive intention, you're like a captain navigating your ship through the waters of life, charting a course toward fulfillment and happiness.

Morning Rituals for Positive Energy

Now, let's talk about morning rituals—those sacred moments that kickstart your day on a positive note. Whether it's a few minutes of meditation, a gratitude practice, or a dance party in your pajamas (yes, you read that right!), morning rituals are your secret weapon for infusing positive energy into your day.

Consider incorporating affirmations into your morning routine. As you sip your coffee or tea, repeat affirmations that align with your intentions for the day. It's like giving yourself a motivational pep talk, and trust me, your soul will thank you for it.

Affirmations for Goal Setting and Achievement

Ah, goals—the stepping stones that lead us toward our dreams. This chapter wouldn't be complete without delving into how positive thinking and affirmations can propel you toward your aspirations.

Affirmations can serve as your cheerleaders on the journey toward your goals. Instead of fixating on potential obstacles or self-doubt, affirmations redirect your focus to your capabilities and the belief that you are fully capable of achieving what you set out to do.

Here are a few goal-oriented affirmations to get you started:

1. *I am a magnet for success, and I attract opportunities that lead me to my goals.*
2. *I trust in my ability to achieve my dreams and overcome any obstacles in my path.*
3. *Every step I take is a step toward my goals, and I am making progress every day.*
4. *I am worthy of the success and abundance that comes with achieving my goals.*

Remember, friend, your goals are not just distant destinations; they're the scenic stops along the journey of your incredible life.

Embracing the Journey

As we wrap up this chapter on the power of positive thinking, I want you to take a moment to appreciate the journey you're embarking on. This isn't about perfection or having it all figured out. It's about embracing the process, the beautiful messiness of life, and the potential for growth and fulfillment that lies ahead.

So, let those positive thoughts bloom, my friend. Affirmations are the water that nourishes the seeds of your mind, and each day is a new opportunity to cultivate a garden of positivity and joy. In the next chapters, we'll explore even more facets of your amazing self, diving into the realms of self-love, gratitude, healthy relationships, and so much more.

Get ready for a daily dose of wisdom whispers that will accompany you on this incredible journey toward a more fulfilling life. I'm honored to be your guide, and I can't wait to see the magic unfold in the chapters to come.

Cheers to positive thinking, setting intentions, and the fulfilling life that awaits you! Until next time, keep those thoughts shining bright.

CHAPTER 2. BUILDING A FOUNDATION FOR SUCCESS

Hey there, marvelous soul! Welcome to the second chapter of "Wisdom Whispers: Daily Affirmations for a Fulfilling Life." I'm absolutely thrilled to continue this journey of positivity and self-discovery with you. In this chapter, we're diving into the art of "Building a Foundation for Success." Get ready to uncover the secrets to setting the stage for a day filled with joy, accomplishment, and positivity.

Setting Intentions for the Day

Alright, let's kick things off by talking about the power of intentions. Ever notice how the first few moments of your day can shape the entire narrative that unfolds? It's like the opening scene of your favorite movie—it sets the mood, the vibe, and gives you a glimpse of what's to come.

Why Intention Matters: Setting intentions for the day is like creating a roadmap for your journey. It's about consciously deciding how you want to navigate the twists and turns that life might throw your way. Instead of being tossed around by the currents of circumstance, you become the captain of your ship, steering towards joy, success, and fulfillment.

How to Set Positive Intentions: Start your day by taking a few quiet moments to connect with yourself. Close your eyes, take a deep breath, and let your mind settle. Ask yourself, "How do I want to feel today? What energy do I want to bring into my day?" Your intention could be as simple as "Today, I choose joy" or "I am open to the possibilities that today brings."

Affirmations for Setting Intentions: To supercharge this practice, incorporate affirmations that align with your daily intentions. For example:

1. *"Today, I choose to embrace joy in every moment."*
2. *"I am open to the opportunities that come my way today."*
3. *"My day is filled with positivity, and I attract success effortlessly."*

Remember, intentions are like the North Star guiding your day. They help you stay aligned with your goals and create an atmosphere of positivity around you.

Morning Rituals for Positive Energy

Now, let's talk about morning rituals—those sacred moments that can set the tone for the entire day. Your morning routine is your personal launching pad, propelling you into a day filled with positive energy, focus, and purpose.

Why Morning Rituals Matter: Picture this: You wake up, stretch, and instead of immediately diving into the demands of the day, you carve out time for yourself. Whether it's a few minutes of meditation, a gratitude practice, or a dance party in your living room (yes, you read that right!), morning rituals infuse your day with positivity and set the stage for success.

Creating Your Morning Ritual: Your morning ritual is entirely yours, so make it something you look forward to. It could involve activities that bring you joy, peace, or a sense of accomplishment. Here are a few ideas to get you started:

1. *Meditation or mindfulness exercises to center your mind.*
2. *Expressing gratitude for the small joys in your life.*
3. *Setting your intentions for the day with positive affirmations.*
4. *Physical activities like stretching or a quick workout to energize your body.*

Affirmations for Morning Rituals: Infuse your morning ritual with affirmations that resonate with you. As you engage in your chosen activities, repeat affirmations that align with your intentions for the day. Here are some examples:

1. *"I am ready to embrace the opportunities this day holds."*
2. *"My day begins with positivity, setting the stage for success."*
3. *"I am grateful for the gift of a new day and the endless possibilities it brings."*

Your morning ritual is your personal ceremony of self-love, a powerful reminder that you are worthy of dedicating time to your well-being.

Affirmations for Goal Setting and Achievement

Ah, goals—the compass that guides us on our journey of self-discovery and fulfillment. In this section, we'll explore how positive thinking and affirmations can turbocharge your pursuit of success.

Why Goals and Affirmations Go Hand in Hand: Goals give our lives direction, purpose, and a sense of accomplishment. When paired with affirmations, they become even more potent. Affirmations infuse your goals with positive energy, helping you overcome self-doubt, stay focused, and navigate obstacles with resilience.

Crafting Goal-Centric Affirmations: When creating affirmations for your goals, keep them specific, positive, and in the present tense. This helps to reprogram your subconscious mind and reinforce your belief in your ability to achieve those goals. Here are a few examples:

1. *"I am confidently moving towards my goals, knowing that I have what it takes to succeed."*

2. *"Every step I take brings me closer to the achievement of my dreams."*
3. *"I trust in my ability to overcome challenges and reach my goals with ease."*

Visualizing Success with Affirmations:

Visualization is a powerful technique to complement your affirmations. As you repeat your affirmations, visualize yourself achieving your goals. Imagine the emotions, the sights, and the sounds associated with your success. This creates a vivid mental image that strengthens your belief in your capabilities.

Remember, your goals are not just distant destinations; they are the scenic stops along the beautiful journey of your life.

Embracing the Journey

As we wrap up this exploration of building a foundation for success, I want you to take a moment to appreciate the journey you're on. It's not just about reaching the destination; it's about the growth, the learning, and the person you become along the way.

Affirmations as Your Daily Allies: Affirmations are your companions on this journey. They're the whispers of encouragement that remind you of your strength, resilience, and worthiness. Whether you're setting intentions, engaging in morning rituals, or chasing your goals, affirmations are there to amplify the positive energy surrounding you.

Consistency is Key: Building a foundation for success is not a one-time task; it's a daily practice. Consistency is the secret sauce that turns positive thinking and affirmations into powerful habits. The more you infuse these practices into your daily routine, the more they become a natural part of who you are.

Celebrate Small Wins: Success isn't always about grand achievements; it's often found in the small victories along the way. Celebrate your progress, no matter how incremental. Each step forward is a testament to your strength and determination.

Affirmations as Daily Reminders: As you continue your journey, let affirmations be your daily reminders of your potential, your resilience, and your worthiness. Here's a closing affirmation to carry with you:

"I am on a journey of growth and fulfillment. Each day, I build a foundation for success with positivity, intention, and the belief in my limitless potential. I am worthy of all the success and joy that comes my way."

So, my incredible friend, keep building that foundation for success. The best is yet to come, and I'm honored to be a part of your journey. Until the next chapter, embrace the positive energy, set those intentions, and celebrate the magic of your journey toward a more fulfilling life. Cheers to you!

CHAPTER 3. NURTURING SELF-LOVE AND CONFIDENCE

Hello, wonderful soul! Welcome to the heartwarming embrace of Chapter 3 in "Wisdom Whispers: Daily Affirmations for a Fulfilling Life." Today, we're delving into the transformative world of "Nurturing Self-Love and Confidence." So, grab a cozy blanket, settle in, and let's explore how affirmations can become your daily companions on the journey to embracing yourself with love and radiating confidence.

The Role of Self-Love in Personal Growth

Let's kick things off by diving into the magical realm of self-love. It's not just a buzzword; it's the secret sauce that nourishes your soul and propels you toward personal growth. Self-love is the foundation upon which confidence, resilience, and fulfillment thrive.

Why Self-Love Matters: Imagine yourself as a garden, and self-love is the sunlight that bathes you in warmth and the rain that nourishes your roots. When you cultivate self-love, you create an environment where you can blossom into the fullest expression of yourself. It's about recognizing your worthiness, embracing your imperfections, and treating yourself with the kindness and compassion you deserve.

Affirmations as Seeds of Self-Love: Affirmations play a crucial role in nurturing self-love. They're like tiny seeds planted in the garden of your mind, gradually blossoming into a lush landscape of positivity. Here are some affirmations to kickstart your journey into the world of self-love:

1. *"I am deserving of love and respect, starting with the love I give to myself."*
2. *"I embrace my flaws and imperfections, for they are a beautiful part of who I am."*
3. *"My worth is inherent, and I am enough just as I am."*

Affirmations for Boosting Self-Confidence

Now, let's turn our attention to another superhero in the realm of personal growth—self-confidence. Confidence is the fuel that propels you to take on challenges, pursue your dreams, and navigate life with grace and poise.

The Dance of Confidence and Affirmations:
Confidence isn't about perfection; it's about embracing your strengths, acknowledging your achievements, and stepping into your power. Affirmations become your dance partner in this journey, reinforcing the belief in your abilities and reminding you of your inherent value.

Affirmations for a Confidence Boost:
1. *"I trust in my ability to handle any challenges that come my way."*
2. *"Every step I take builds my confidence, and I am growing stronger every day."*
3. *"I am a magnet for positive opportunities, and I approach them with confidence and enthusiasm."*

Embracing Affirmations as Daily Practices:
Incorporate affirmations into your daily routine to supercharge your confidence. Whether you say them aloud in front of the mirror, jot them down in a journal, or repeat them silently during moments of self-

reflection, affirmations become the soundtrack to your journey of building unshakable confidence.

Celebrating Personal Strengths

Now, let's take a moment to celebrate your personal strengths. Each of us possesses a unique set of qualities, skills, and talents that make us extraordinary. It's time to shine a spotlight on these strengths and let them illuminate your path.

The Power of Acknowledging Strengths: Acknowledging your strengths isn't about boasting; it's about recognizing the incredible gifts you bring to the world. Your strengths are the tools in your toolkit, ready to be wielded as you navigate the twists and turns of life.

Affirmations to Celebrate Strengths:

1. *"I celebrate my unique strengths and the positive impact they have on my life and others."*
2. *"My strengths are a source of empowerment, guiding me toward success and fulfillment."*

3. *"I am continually discovering new strengths within myself, and I embrace them with gratitude."*

Affirmations as Personal Pep Talks: Use affirmations as personal pep talks to remind yourself of your strengths during challenging moments. When faced with a task that seems daunting, repeat affirmations that highlight your capabilities and the strengths you possess to overcome obstacles.

The Dance of Self-Love and Confidence

As we navigate the dance between self-love and confidence, it's essential to understand that they are intertwined, each influencing and amplifying the other. When you love yourself, you naturally exude confidence, and when you embrace confidence, you cultivate a deeper well of self-love.

Affirmations to Merge Self-Love and Confidence:

1. *"I love and accept myself unconditionally, and this love empowers my confidence."*

2. *"My confidence is a reflection of the deep well of self-love within me."*

3. *"With each affirmation, I strengthen the bond between my self-love and confidence."*

Affirmations as Daily Rituals: Make affirmations a part of your daily rituals. Start your day by acknowledging your worth and capabilities. Let these affirmations become the soundtrack that sets the tone for a day filled with self-love and confidence.

Embracing and Celebrating Personal Strengths

Now, let's take a moment to celebrate your personal strengths. Each of us possesses a unique set of qualities, skills, and talents that make us extraordinary. It's time to shine a spotlight on these strengths and let them illuminate your path.

The Power of Acknowledging Strengths: Acknowledging your strengths isn't about boasting; it's about recognizing the incredible gifts you bring to the world. Your strengths are the tools in your toolkit, ready to be wielded as you navigate the twists and turns of life.

Affirmations to Celebrate Strengths:

1. *"I celebrate my unique strengths and the positive impact they have on my life and others."*

2. *"My strengths are a source of empowerment, guiding me toward success and fulfillment."*

3. *"I am continually discovering new strengths within myself, and I embrace them with gratitude."*

Affirmations as Personal Pep Talks: Use affirmations as personal pep talks to remind yourself of your strengths during challenging moments. When faced with a task that seems daunting, repeat affirmations that highlight your capabilities and the strengths you possess to overcome obstacles.

Embracing the Dance of Self-Love and Confidence

As we navigate the dance between self-love and confidence, it's essential to understand that they are intertwined, each influencing and amplifying the other.

When you love yourself, you naturally exude confidence, and when you embrace confidence, you cultivate a deeper well of self-love.

Affirmations to Merge Self-Love and Confidence:

1. *"I love and accept myself unconditionally, and this love empowers my confidence."*
2. *"My confidence is a reflection of the deep well of self-love within me."*
3. *"With each affirmation, I strengthen the bond between my self-love and confidence."*

Affirmations as Daily Rituals: Make affirmations a part of your daily rituals. Start your day by acknowledging your worth and capabilities. Let these affirmations become the soundtrack that sets the tone for a day filled with self-love and confidence.

Embracing the Journey

As we wrap up this exploration of self-love and confidence, I want to leave you with an affirmation to carry with you on your journey:

"I am a radiant being, overflowing with self-love and confidence. Each day, I celebrate the unique tapestry of strengths within me, embracing myself with kindness and believing in my boundless potential. I am a beacon of love and confidence, and my journey is a dance of joy and fulfillment."

So, my incredible friend, keep dancing to the rhythm of self-love and confidence. Affirmations are your partners in this beautiful journey, reminding you that you are worthy, you are capable, and you are enough. Until the next chapter, embrace the love within you, stand tall in your confidence, and celebrate the magic that is uniquely you. You've got this!

CHAPTER 4. CULTIVATING GRATITUDE

Hey there, fabulous soul! Welcome to Chapter 4 of "Wisdom Whispers: Daily Affirmations for a Fulfilling Life." Today, we're diving into the transformative and heartwarming world of "Cultivating Gratitude." Get ready to embark on a journey that will shift your perspective, fill your heart with warmth, and infuse your life with positivity.

The Power of Gratitude

Gratitude—it's like a magical elixir for the soul. When you sprinkle gratitude into your life, it transforms the ordinary into the extraordinary. This chapter is all about uncovering the incredible power of gratitude and how daily affirmations can be the key to cultivating a grateful heart.

Why Gratitude Matters: Gratitude isn't just a fleeting emotion; it's a way of life. It's the practice of recognizing and appreciating the goodness in your life, both big and small. When you cultivate gratitude, you open the door to a myriad of benefits—improved mood, reduced stress, enhanced relationships, and an overall sense of well-being.

The Ripple Effect of Gratitude: Gratitude has this beautiful ripple effect. When you express gratitude, it not only uplifts your own spirit but also has the power to positively impact those around you. It's like tossing a pebble into a pond—the ripples extend far beyond the point of impact.

Daily Affirmations for Gratitude Practice

Now, let's explore how affirmations can be your guiding light on the path of gratitude. Affirmations are like love notes to the universe, expressing your appreciation for the abundance in your life. They're a gentle reminder to focus on the good, even in the midst of challenges.

Affirmations for Gratitude:

1. *"I am grateful for the abundance that flows into my life in unexpected ways."*
2. *"My heart is filled with gratitude for the simple joys that bring me happiness."*

3. *"I appreciate the lessons hidden within challenges, knowing they lead to growth."*

Morning Affirmations for Gratitude:

Incorporate gratitude affirmations into your morning routine. As you sip your coffee or tea, take a moment to express gratitude for the new day and the opportunities it holds.

1. *"I am thankful for the gift of a new day, filled with endless possibilities."*
2. *"Gratitude is my morning ritual, setting the tone for a positive and joyful day."*
3. *"I start my day with a grateful heart, attracting even more blessings into my life."*

Evening Affirmations for Gratitude: Wrap up your day with gratitude. Reflect on the moments that brought you joy and the lessons learned. Here are a few affirmations to guide your evening reflections:

1. *"I am grateful for the experiences that brought me growth and wisdom today."*
2. *"My heart overflows with gratitude for the love and support that surrounds me."*

3. *"As I drift into sleep, I am thankful for the beauty woven into the tapestry of my day."*

Transforming Challenges into Opportunities for Growth

Life is a journey of peaks and valleys, and challenges are inevitable companions along the way. However, through the lens of gratitude, challenges become opportunities for growth and resilience.

Affirmations for Transforming Challenges:

1. *"I embrace challenges as stepping stones on my journey, knowing they lead to greater strength."*
2. *"In the face of adversity, I am grateful for the lessons that shape my character."*
3. *"Every challenge is an opportunity for me to rise and shine, and I am grateful for the chance to do so."*

Shifting Perspective with Affirmations:

Affirmations have the power to shift your perspective on challenges. Instead of viewing them as roadblocks, affirmations help you see them as detours guiding you to unexpected beauty and growth.

Affirmations for Shifting Perspective:

1. *"I trust that challenges are guiding me toward a better version of myself."*
2. *"My perspective shapes my reality, and I choose to see challenges as opportunities."*
3. *"I am resilient, and challenges only strengthen my capacity for joy and gratitude."*

Gratitude in Relationships

Now, let's explore how gratitude can be a game-changer in your relationships. Whether with friends, family, or your significant other, expressing gratitude fosters connection, deepens bonds, and creates a positive atmosphere.

Affirmations for Relationship Gratitude:

1. *"I am grateful for the love and support that flows between me and my loved ones."*
2. *"Expressing gratitude deepens my relationships and brings joy to both me and others."*
3. *"In every interaction, I find something to be thankful for, strengthening the ties that bind us."*

Affirmations for Self-Love within Relationships: Remember, gratitude for others starts with self-love. Affirmations can be a powerful tool for nurturing self-love within the context of relationships.

1. *"I deserve love and appreciation in my relationships, and I am grateful for the love I receive."*

2. *"My relationships are a reflection of the love I have for myself, and I am worthy of that love."*

3. *"I attract positive and fulfilling relationships into my life, and I am thankful for each connection."*

Gratitude as a Lifestyle

Gratitude isn't a one-time event; it's a lifestyle. It's about weaving a thread of appreciation into the fabric of your daily existence. Affirmations become the stitches that hold this thread in place, creating a beautiful tapestry of gratitude.

Affirmations for a Gratitude Lifestyle:

1. *"Gratitude is my daily practice, enhancing the richness of my life."*

2. *"I choose to see the world through the lens of gratitude, attracting positivity and abundance."*

3. *"My heart is a garden of gratitude, and each affirmation is a blossom that adds to its beauty."*

Affirmations for Spreading Gratitude: Gratitude is contagious, and your practice can inspire others. Affirmations become your tools for spreading the warmth of gratitude to those around you.

1. *"I radiate gratitude, uplifting the spirits of those I encounter."*
2. *"My expressions of gratitude create a positive ripple effect in the world."*
3. *"As I share my gratitude, I inspire others to embrace the beauty of appreciation."*

Embracing the Journey

As we conclude this exploration of gratitude and affirmations, let's carry a special affirmation with us:

"I am a grateful being, and my life is a tapestry woven with threads of appreciation. Each day, I embrace the beauty in every moment, transforming challenges into opportunities and relationships into bonds of love. Gratitude is my guide, and affirmations are my daily expressions of appreciation, shaping a life filled with joy and fulfillment."

So, dear friend, let gratitude be your constant companion on this journey. Affirmations are the keys to unlocking the door to a life adorned with gratitude. Until the next chapter, may your heart be filled with thanks, and may you continue to discover the magic hidden in the everyday moments of your extraordinary life. Cheers to you and the beautiful journey ahead!

CHAPTER 5. CREATING HEALTHY RELATIONSHIPS

Hello, wonderful soul! Welcome to Chapter 5 of "Wisdom Whispers: Daily Affirmations for a Fulfilling Life." Today, we're diving into the realm of "Creating Healthy Relationships." Relationships are the vibrant threads that weave the tapestry of our lives, and in this chapter, we'll explore how daily affirmations can be the guiding stars in nurturing connections, fostering understanding, and creating a space for love to flourish.

The Dance of Connection

Relationships are the heartbeat of our human experience—a dance of connection, understanding, and shared moments. In this chapter, we'll unravel the secrets of creating healthy relationships, with affirmations as our compass.

The Essence of Healthy Relationships: Healthy relationships are like well-tended gardens; they require care, attention, and the nourishment of positive energy.

They're spaces where individuals grow, support each other, and find solace in the shared journey.

Affirmations as Building Blocks: Affirmations become the building blocks of healthy relationships. They lay the foundation for communication, understanding, and the nurturing of love. Let's explore how affirmations can infuse your relationships with positivity and create an environment for growth.

Affirmations for Communication

Communication is the lifeline of any relationship, and positive, affirming words can create a bridge of understanding and connection.

Affirmations for Positive Communication:
1. *"I communicate with kindness, openness, and honesty, fostering a safe space for connection."*
2. *"My words are a reflection of love, respect, and the intention to understand and be understood."*
3. *"I listen with empathy, seeking to understand before being understood."*

Affirmations for Conflict Resolution: Conflict is a natural part of relationships, but it's how we navigate it that defines the health of the connection.

1. *"I approach conflicts with a spirit of understanding, seeking resolutions that strengthen our bond."*

2. *"Our disagreements are opportunities for growth, and I navigate them with patience and compassion."*

3. *"I communicate my needs and boundaries with clarity and respect, fostering mutual understanding."*

Nurturing Self-Love within Relationships

Before we can fully contribute to a healthy relationship, we must cultivate self-love. Affirmations can be powerful tools in nurturing self-love within the context of relationships.

Affirmations for Self-Love within Relationships:

1. *"I deserve love and respect in my relationships, and I am worthy of healthy connections."*

2. *"My self-worth is independent of external opinions, and I love and honor myself within my relationships."*

3. *"I attract relationships that align with my values and contribute positively to my growth and well-being."*

Affirmations for Boundaries: Setting and maintaining healthy boundaries is a crucial aspect of any relationship.

1. *"I communicate and uphold my boundaries with love and firmness, creating a space of mutual respect."*

2. *"Boundaries are an expression of self-love, and I honor them for the well-being of myself and my relationships."*

3. *"In respecting my own boundaries, I teach others to do the same, fostering harmony within my relationships."*

Affirmations for Gratitude in Relationships

Gratitude is the sweet nectar that keeps relationships blooming. Expressing appreciation through affirmations creates a positive loop of love and connection.

Affirmations for Gratitude in Relationships:

1. *"I am grateful for the love and support that flows between me and my loved ones."*
2. *"Every day, I express gratitude for the unique qualities that make our relationship special."*
3. *"My heart is a garden of gratitude, and I water it daily with affirmations of appreciation."*

Affirmations for Love and Connection:

Affirmations can deepen the bonds of love and connection within relationships.

1. *"Love is the foundation of my relationships, and I nurture it with daily affirmations of appreciation."*
2. *"I am open to giving and receiving love, creating a cycle of connection and warmth within my relationships."*

3. *"The love within me attracts love into my relationships, creating a tapestry of connection and understanding."*

Building a Shared Vision

Healthy relationships often involve aligning values and creating a shared vision for the future. Affirmations can be the guideposts that lead the way.

Affirmations for a Shared Vision:

1. *"We share a vision for the future built on love, mutual growth, and shared values."*
2. *"Our individual goals align to create a harmonious and fulfilling shared vision for our journey together."*
3. *"Through open communication and affirmation, we build a future that honors both our individual dreams and our shared aspirations."*

Embracing the Journey

As we wrap up this exploration of creating healthy relationships, let's carry a special affirmation with us:

"I am a builder of healthy relationships, and each affirmation is a brick in the foundation of love, understanding, and connection. I communicate with kindness, navigate conflicts with grace, and nurture self-love within the context of my relationships. Every day, I express gratitude for the unique qualities that make each connection special, creating a tapestry of love that enriches my life."

So, my incredible friend, may your relationships be filled with love, understanding, and positive affirmations. Until the next chapter, keep building those healthy connections, embracing the dance of love, and celebrating the magic that unfolds within the tapestry of your relationships. Cheers to you and the beautiful journey ahead!

Chapter 6. Embracing Change and Resilience

Hello, resilient soul! Welcome to Chapter 6 of "Wisdom Whispers: Daily Affirmations for a Fulfilling Life." Today, we're diving into the dynamic and transformative world of "Embracing Change and Resilience." Life is a journey filled with twists, turns, and unexpected detours, and in this chapter, we'll explore how daily affirmations can be your companions on the road to embracing change with grace and cultivating unwavering resilience.

The Dance of Change

Change is the only constant in life, a rhythm that plays in the background of our journey. In this chapter, we'll unravel the dance of change and resilience, discovering how affirmations can be the rhythm that guides our steps.

The Nature of Change: Change is a natural part of the human experience. It can be exhilarating, challenging, and sometimes, a bit overwhelming.

Whether it's a change in circumstances, relationships, or personal growth, our ability to navigate change determines our resilience and adaptability.

Affirmations as Anchors in Change: Affirmations serve as anchors when the seas of change become tumultuous. They provide a steady foundation, reminding us of our strength, adaptability, and the potential for growth in every new experience.

Affirmations for Embracing Change

Change often brings a mix of excitement and discomfort. Affirmations can be your allies in navigating the waves of change with a positive mindset.

Affirmations for Embracing Change:

1. *"I embrace change as a natural and necessary part of my journey, bringing new opportunities for growth."*
2. *"Change is a catalyst for transformation, and I welcome the positive shifts it brings into my life."*
3. *"I am adaptable and resilient, capable of navigating change with grace and a positive attitude."*

Affirmations for Flexibility: Flexibility is a key element in embracing change. Affirmations can help cultivate a flexible mindset that bends but doesn't break.

1. *"I am like a tree in the wind, flexible and grounded, swaying with the changes but standing tall."*

2. *"Change allows me to stretch beyond my comfort zone, discovering new aspects of my strength and resilience."*

3. *"Flexibility is my superpower, and it empowers me to adapt to any changes that come my way."*

Cultivating Resilience

Resilience is the ability to bounce back from adversity, to rise stronger after facing challenges. Affirmations become the mantras that strengthen your resilience muscle.

Affirmations for Resilience:

1. *"I am resilient, and every challenge I face is an opportunity for personal and spiritual growth."*

2. *"In the face of adversity, I stand firm, knowing that I have the strength to overcome any obstacle."*

3. *"Resilience is my birthright, and I embrace it as a powerful force within me."*

Affirmations for Learning from Challenges:

Challenges are not setbacks; they are lessons in disguise. Affirmations can help shift your perspective and extract wisdom from every experience.

1. *"Every challenge is an opportunity for me to learn, grow, and become more resilient."*

2. *"I find strength in adversity, and each challenge is a stepping stone on my journey to success."*

3. *"Challenges are my teachers, and I approach them with an open heart and a willingness to learn."*

Affirmations for Self-Compassion

Change and challenges often come with a range of emotions. Self-compassion is the gentle reminder that it's okay not to be okay.

Affirmations for Self-Compassion:

1. *"I am kind to myself during times of change, understanding that it's okay to feel a range of emotions."*

2. *"Self-compassion is my anchor in the storm of change, allowing me to navigate with grace and acceptance."*

3. *"I honor my feelings and emotions, recognizing them as valid and essential components of my human experience."*

Affirmations for Self-Love in Change: Change provides an opportunity for self-discovery and self-love. Affirmations can be the mirror that reflects your worthiness.

1. *"I love and accept myself in the midst of change, knowing that I am worthy of love and understanding."*

2. *"Change is an opportunity for self-growth, and I embrace it with love and an open heart."*

3. *"My worth is not defined by external circumstances; I am inherently valuable, no matter the changes around me."*

Affirmations for Embracing the Unknown

Change often leads us into the territory of the unknown. Affirmations can be the guiding stars that illuminate the path forward.

Affirmations for Embracing the Unknown:

1. *"I step into the unknown with courage and curiosity, trusting that it holds the seeds of new opportunities."*

2. *"The unknown is a canvas of possibilities, and I paint my journey with the colors of hope and excitement."*

3. *"Change is my ally, and the unknown is my playground for exploration and self-discovery."*

Affirmations for Trust: Trust is the bridge that connects you to the other side of change. Affirmations can build and reinforce that bridge.

1. *"I trust in the process of life, and I know that even in the face of change, I am guided and supported."*

2. *"Change is a testament to my growth, and I trust that it aligns with the greater plan for my journey."*

3.   *"In times of uncertainty, I trust myself, my*
     abilities, and the resilience that lies within me."

Embracing the Journey

As we conclude this exploration of embracing change and resilience, let's carry a special affirmation with us:

"I am a resilient being, capable of embracing change with grace and positivity. Affirmations are my companions on the journey, providing me with strength, flexibility, and self-compassion. In the face of challenges, I rise stronger, and in the unknown, I find opportunities for growth and self-discovery. Change is not a threat; it's a canvas for me to paint my story of resilience and triumph."

So, dear friend, may you navigate the dance of change with courage, resilience, and the uplifting power of affirmations. Until the next chapter, embrace the unknown with open arms, celebrate your strength in the face of challenges, and dance through the changes with a heart filled with resilience. Cheers to you and the beautiful journey ahead!

CHAPTER 7. MINDFULNESS AND INNER PEACE

Hello, serene soul! Welcome to Chapter 7 of "Wisdom Whispers: Daily Affirmations for a Fulfilling Life." Today, we're immersing ourselves in the tranquil and transformative world of "Mindfulness and Inner Peace." In this chapter, we'll explore how daily affirmations can be your guides to cultivating mindfulness, embracing the present moment, and finding that inner sanctuary of peace that resides within you.

The Essence of Mindfulness

Mindfulness is more than a practice; it's a way of being. It's the art of living fully in the present moment, savoring the richness of each experience without being entangled in the past or the future. In this chapter, we'll uncover the beauty of mindfulness and how affirmations can be the gentle reminders to anchor us in the now.

The Gift of the Present Moment: Our lives unfold in the present moment, yet so often, our minds drift to the past or leap into the future. Mindfulness is the gift of presence, allowing us to savor the beauty, joy, and lessons that each moment offers.

Affirmations as Anchors in the Now:
Affirmations serve as anchors in the present moment, gently guiding our attention back to the now. They remind us to breathe, observe, and fully engage with the tapestry of life as it unfolds.

Affirmations for Cultivating Mindfulness

Mindfulness is a practice, and affirmations can be your companions on this journey. They infuse your awareness with intention, guiding you to fully experience each moment with clarity and presence.

Affirmations for Present-Moment Awareness:
1. *"I am fully present in this moment, embracing the beauty that surrounds me."*
2. *"My awareness is a gift, and I use it to fully engage with the richness of each experience."*

3. *"In the stillness of the present moment, I find peace, joy, and a profound sense of connection."*

Affirmations for Breath Awareness: The breath is a sacred anchor to the present moment. Affirmations can deepen your connection to the rhythmic dance of inhalation and exhalation.

1. *"I breathe in calmness, and I exhale tension, grounding myself in the beauty of the present."*
2. *"With each breath, I connect to the essence of life, finding serenity in the here and now."*
3. *"My breath is a reminder of the miracle of existence, and I honor it with mindful awareness."*

Cultivating Inner Peace

Inner peace is not the absence of challenges; it's the ability to remain centered in the midst of them. Affirmations become the mantras that guide you to the tranquil center within.

Affirmations for Inner Peace:

1. *"I carry a serene sanctuary within me, accessible at any moment through mindful presence."*

2. *"No matter the external chaos, I am a pillar of peace, grounded in the tranquility of my inner being."*

3. *"Peace resides within me, and I nurture it through mindful awareness and self-compassion."*

Affirmations for Letting Go: Mindfulness involves letting go of attachments to the past or worries about the future. Affirmations can be the keys to releasing what no longer serves you.

1. *"I release the past with gratitude, and I step into the present with an open heart."*

2. *"The future is a blank canvas, and I paint it with the colors of my mindful presence."*

3. *"In letting go of expectations, I create space for serenity and peace to blossom."*

Affirmations for Gratitude in the Present

The present moment is a treasure trove of experiences, and affirmations can help you unwrap the gifts it offers. Gratitude becomes the bridge that connects you to the beauty of the now.

Affirmations for Present-Moment Gratitude:

1. *"I am grateful for the small miracles that unfold in the present moment, filling my heart with joy."*

2. *"Gratitude is my companion in the here and now, amplifying the beauty of each experience."*

3. *"In this moment, I find an abundance of reasons to be grateful, and I express my thanks with an open heart."*

Affirmations for Sensory Awareness:

Mindfulness involves engaging all your senses in the present experience. Affirmations can heighten your sensory awareness, enriching your connection to the world around you.

1. *"I savor the taste of each bite, the textures beneath my fingers, and the symphony of sounds around me."*

2. *"My senses are gateways to the richness of life, and I engage them fully to experience the present moment."*

3. *"In this moment, I am fully present, seeing, hearing, smelling, tasting, and feeling the beauty that surrounds me."*

Mindfulness in Daily Activities

Mindfulness isn't confined to meditation; it's a way of infusing awareness into daily activities. Affirmations can be your reminders to bring mindfulness into every aspect of your life.

Affirmations for Mindful Eating:

1. *"I eat with awareness, savoring each bite and nourishing my body with gratitude."*
2. *"In the act of eating, I find a sacred communion with the nourishment that sustains me."*
3. *"I am mindful of the flavors, textures, and sensations as I eat, fully present in this nourishing moment."*

Affirmations for Mindful Walking: Walking becomes a meditation when done with mindfulness. Affirmations can guide your steps with intention.

1. *"With each step, I am grounded in the present moment, feeling the earth beneath me."*
2. *"Walking is a dance with the present, and I move with mindful awareness, fully engaged in each stride."*

3. *"I walk with purpose, appreciating the simple joy of movement and the rhythm of my breath."*

Affirmations for Mindful Relationships

Mindfulness extends to your connections with others. Affirmations can deepen the quality of your relationships by fostering presence and understanding.

Affirmations for Mindful Relationships:

1. *"I am fully present in my relationships, listening with an open heart and engaging with genuine compassion."*
2. *"Mindful awareness enhances the depth and authenticity of my connections with others."*
3. *"In conversations, I am present, offering my full attention and creating space for understanding and connection."*

Affirmations for Compassionate Listening:

Mindful listening is a form of compassion. Affirmations can guide you to listen with an open heart and empathetic understanding.

1. *"I listen with compassion, hearing not only the words but also the emotions and intentions behind them."*
2. *"In moments of conversation, I am present and attentive, creating a space for genuine connection."*
3. *"My mindful listening fosters understanding and strengthens the bonds of love and connection in my relationships."*

Embracing the Journey

As we conclude this exploration of mindfulness and inner peace, let's carry a special affirmation with us:

"I am a mindful being, and each affirmation is a gentle guide to the present moment, where I find peace, joy, and a profound sense of connection. I cultivate mindfulness in every aspect of my life, savoring the richness of each experience. In the embrace of the present moment, I discover the sanctuary of inner peace that resides within me."

So, dear friend, may you walk the path of mindfulness with grace, savoring each moment and finding tranquility within. Until the next chapter, may your journey be filled with the serenity of the present, and may your heart be a sanctuary of inner peace. Cheers to you and the beautiful journey ahead!

CHAPTER 8. AFFIRMATIONS FOR HEALTH AND WELL-BEING

Hello, radiant soul! Welcome to Chapter 8 of "Wisdom Whispers: Daily Affirmations for a Fulfilling Life." Today, we're delving into the nurturing and empowering realm of "Affirmations for Health and Well-being." In this chapter, we'll explore how daily affirmations can be your allies on the journey to vibrant health, embracing wellness as a holistic and harmonious aspect of your life.

The Harmony of Health and Well-being

Health and well-being are the threads that weave through the fabric of a fulfilling life. In this chapter, we'll discover the transformative power of affirmations, crafting words that resonate with the energy of vitality, balance, and a deep sense of well-being.

The Holistic Nature of Well-being: Well-being extends beyond physical health; it encompasses mental, emotional, and spiritual harmony. Affirmations become the brushstrokes that paint a holistic masterpiece of well-being in every aspect of your life.

Affirmations as Seeds of Well-being:
Affirmations are like seeds planted in the garden of your mind. As you nurture them with intention and belief, they blossom into a tapestry of well-being that radiates throughout your entire being.

Affirmations for Physical Health

Physical health is the foundation on which the temple of well-being stands. Affirmations become the pillars that support your journey to vitality and balance.

Affirmations for Vitality:

1. *"I am a vessel of vibrant health, and my body radiates with boundless energy."*
2. *"Every cell in my body is infused with vitality and the healing power of well-being."*
3. *"I nourish my body with wholesome foods, and it responds with strength, vitality, and perfect health."*

Affirmations for Healing: Affirmations can be potent tools for invoking the body's natural healing mechanisms.

1. *"My body is a temple of healing, and I trust in its innate ability to restore and rejuvenate."*
2. *"I am surrounded by healing energy, and it flows through me, promoting health and well-being."*
3. *"With each breath, I inhale healing energy, and with each exhale, I release any tension or discomfort."*

Affirmations for Mental Well-being

A healthy mind is the cornerstone of well-being. Affirmations become the gentle whispers that guide your thoughts toward positivity, clarity, and mental harmony.

Affirmations for Positive Thinking:

1. *"My mind is a sanctuary of positive thoughts, creating a harmonious environment for well-being."*
2. *"I choose thoughts that uplift, inspire, and contribute to my mental and emotional health."*

3. *"Positive thinking is my natural state of mind, and it nurtures my overall well-being."*

Affirmations for Mental Clarity: A clear and focused mind is a key to overall well-being. Affirmations can be the catalysts for mental clarity.

1. *"I release mental fog and embrace mental clarity, allowing my thoughts to flow with ease."*
2. *"My mind is sharp, focused, and capable of handling any challenges that come my way."*
3. *"Each breath brings clarity to my mind, and I approach life's situations with a calm and focused perspective."*

Affirmations for Emotional Well-being

Emotional well-being is the art of navigating the ebb and flow of emotions with grace and self-awareness. Affirmations become the compass that guides you through the landscape of your emotions.

Affirmations for Emotional Balance:

1. *"I embrace the full spectrum of my emotions, finding balance and wisdom in each experience."*

2. *"Emotional well-being is my birthright, and I navigate my feelings with grace and self-compassion."*

3. *"In moments of emotional turbulence, I breathe and find my center, bringing balance to my heart and soul."*

Affirmations for Self-Compassion: Self-compassion is the gentle embrace that soothes the heart. Affirmations can be the gentle reminders to treat yourself with kindness and understanding.

1. *"I am worthy of love and compassion, especially from myself, in moments of joy and challenge alike."*

2. *"Self-compassion is the foundation of my emotional well-being, and I offer it generously to myself."*

3. *"In times of emotional turbulence, I am gentle with myself, recognizing that I am doing the best I can."*

Affirmations for Spiritual Well-being

Spiritual well-being is the connection to something greater than oneself. Affirmations become the prayers of the soul, fostering a sense of purpose, peace, and transcendence.

Affirmations for Spiritual Connection:

1. *"I am connected to the divine energy that flows through all of existence, guiding me with love and wisdom."*
2. *"Spiritual well-being is the anchor of my soul, grounding me in the awareness of my higher purpose."*
3. *"In moments of stillness, I feel the presence of the divine within and around me, nurturing my spiritual well-being."*

Affirmations for Inner Peace: Inner peace is the gentle hum that resonates within a tranquil heart. Affirmations can be the mantras that lead you to this serene sanctuary.

1. *"I am at peace with the past, present, and future, creating a harmonious space for my well-being."*

2. *"Inner peace is my birthright, and I cultivate it with mindfulness, gratitude, and self-love."*

3. *"My heart is a sanctuary of peace, and I carry this tranquility with me throughout my journey."*

Affirmations for Overall Well-being

Well-being is a symphony of physical, mental, emotional, and spiritual harmony. Affirmations become the music notes that compose this beautiful melody of holistic health.

Affirmations for Holistic Well-being:

1. *"I am a beacon of well-being, radiating health and harmony in body, mind, and spirit."*

2. *"Well-being is my natural state, and I choose thoughts, actions, and habits that support my overall health."*

3. *"Each day, I nurture my well-being with love, gratitude, and choices that align with my highest good."*

Affirmations for Self-Care: Self-care is the foundation of well-being. Affirmations become the affirmations that guide you to prioritize your health and happiness.

1. *"Self-care is a sacred act of love, and I prioritize it in my daily routine for the sake of my well-being."*

2. *"I honor my body, mind, and spirit through conscious self-care practices that support my overall health."*

3. *"My well-being is a priority, and I invest time and energy in activities that nourish and rejuvenate my whole being."*

Embracing the Journey

As we conclude this exploration of affirmations for health and well-being, let's carry a special affirmation with us:

"I am a being of holistic well-being, and each affirmation is a loving guide on my journey to vibrant health and harmony. I nourish my body, cultivate positive thoughts, navigate emotions with grace, and connect with the spiritual essence that flows through me. Well-being is my birthright, and I honor it with daily choices that align with my highest good."

So, dear friend, may your journey be filled with vibrant health, holistic harmony, and a deep sense of well-being. Until the next chapter, may you savor the richness of each moment, embrace the fullness of your emotions, and walk the path of well-being with love and intention. Cheers to you and the beautiful journey ahead!

CHAPTER 9. EVENING REFLECTIONS AND GRATITUDE

Hello, cherished soul! Welcome to Chapter 9 of "Wisdom Whispers: Daily Affirmations for a Fulfilling Life." In this chapter, we're diving into the serene and transformative practice of "Evening Reflections and Gratitude." As the sun sets on another day of your incredible journey, we'll explore how evening reflections and expressions of gratitude through affirmations can become the bridge to a peaceful night and a promising tomorrow.

The Magic of Evening Reflections

Evenings are like the gentle whispers of the universe, inviting you to reflect on the day's moments, learnings, and blessings. In this chapter, we'll uncover the enchantment of evening reflections, understanding how they can be a source of peace, mindfulness, and personal growth.

The Beauty of Reflective Moments: Evening reflections are a sacred pause in the symphony of life, allowing you to appreciate the melody of your experiences, acknowledge challenges, and celebrate victories. It's a moment to embrace the fullness of your day and pave the way for a restful night.

Affirmations as Reflection Guides: Affirmations become your companions in the evening reflections, guiding your thoughts toward gratitude, self-awareness, and the gentle acknowledgment of the day's journey.

Affirmations for Evening Reflections

Affirmations for Acknowledging Challenges:

1. *"I honor the challenges I faced today, recognizing them as opportunities for growth and resilience."*
2. *"In acknowledging the hurdles, I find strength and wisdom that will guide me on my journey."*
3. *"Challenges are stepping stones to success, and I navigate them with courage and a positive mindset."*

Affirmations for Celebrating Victories:

1. *"I celebrate the victories, big and small, that graced my day, acknowledging my progress and achievements."*

2. *"Every triumph is a testament to my capabilities, and I revel in the joy of my accomplishments."*

3. *"My victories are the building blocks of a fulfilling life, and I embrace them with gratitude and humility."*

Affirmations for Gratitude in Reflection:

1. *"I am grateful for the experiences that shaped my day, finding joy in both challenges and triumphs."*

2. *"Gratitude is the gateway to abundance, and I express thanks for the blessings that unfolded today."*

3. *"In reflection, I discover a treasure trove of gratitude, acknowledging the richness of my life's tapestry."*

The Transformative Power of Gratitude

Gratitude is a gentle alchemy that turns everyday moments into precious jewels. In this section, we'll explore how affirmations can be the catalysts for a gratitude practice that illuminates your evenings and sets a positive tone for what lies ahead.

Gratitude as a Daily Ritual: Making gratitude a daily ritual transforms your perspective, inviting you to focus on the positive aspects of your life.

Affirmations for Evening Gratitude:

1. *"I am grateful for the lessons learned today, knowing they contribute to my personal growth."*
2. *"Each day is a gift, and I express gratitude for the opportunities and experiences it brings."*
3. *"Gratitude is my nightly companion, weaving a thread of positivity into the fabric of my thoughts."*

Affirmations for a Peaceful Evening

As the day bids farewell, affirmations can guide you toward a tranquil evening, creating a peaceful space for rest, rejuvenation, and preparation for a new dawn.

Affirmations for Relaxation:

1. *"I release the tension of the day, allowing my body and mind to relax in preparation for a restful night."*
2. *"Evening is a sacred time for relaxation, and I honor it by slowing down and finding moments of calm."*

3. *"My mind unwinds, my body relaxes, and I welcome the serenity that fills the evening air."*

Affirmations for Letting Go:

1. *"I release the events of the day, letting go of any lingering stress or worry."*
2. *"Evening is a time for surrender, and I trust that everything will unfold as it should."*
3. *"As the sun sets, I release the day with gratitude, making space for peace and rejuvenation."*

Affirmations for a Restful Night

A restful night is a gift you give to yourself. Affirmations become the lullabies that soothe your mind and body into a peaceful slumber.

Affirmations for Restful Sleep:

1. *"I welcome a night of deep and restful sleep, knowing it rejuvenates my body, mind, and spirit."*
2. *"My dreams are peaceful, and my sleep is a sanctuary of restoration and healing."*

3. *"As I lay down to sleep, I release any lingering thoughts and surrender to the tranquility of the night."*

Affirmations for a Promising Tomorrow

As the day concludes, affirmations become the whispers of encouragement that shape a promising mindset for the day to come.

Affirmations for a Positive Outlook:

1. *"I look forward to tomorrow with optimism and excitement, knowing that each day is a new opportunity."*

2. *"My mindset is a magnet for positive experiences, and I welcome the opportunities that tomorrow brings."*

3. *"With gratitude for today and hope for tomorrow, I embrace the endless possibilities of my journey."*

Affirmations for Intentions:

1. *"I set positive intentions for tomorrow, aligning my thoughts and actions with my goals and values."*

2. *"Tomorrow is a canvas, and I paint it with the colors of intention, purpose, and positive energy."*
3. *"I am the creator of my tomorrow, and I affirm my ability to shape a day filled with joy and fulfillment."*

Embracing the Journey

As we conclude this exploration of evening reflections and gratitude, let's carry a special affirmation with us:

"I am a grateful being, and each evening, I reflect with gratitude, acknowledging the challenges, celebrating the victories, and expressing thanks for the blessings that unfold. Gratitude is my nightly companion, creating a peaceful space for relaxation, rest, and the promise of a new day. As I lay down to sleep, I release the day with gratitude, knowing that each evening is a bridge to a promising tomorrow."

So, dear friend, may your evenings be filled with reflection, gratitude, and the gentle embrace of peace. Until the next chapter, may your nights be restful, your dreams be sweet, and your mornings be filled with the promise of a new day. Cheers to you and the beautiful journey ahead!

A TAPESTRY OF WISDOM AND FULFILLMENT

Dear kindred spirit, as we reach the final pages of "Wisdom Whispers: Daily Affirmations for a Fulfilling Life," it's with a heart full of gratitude and a sense of fulfillment that we conclude this transformative journey together. This book has been a companion on your path to self-discovery, offering daily affirmations as gentle whispers of wisdom, love, and inspiration. As you reflect on the chapters that unfolded like the petals of a blossoming flower, let's weave together the threads of learning, growth, and the radiant tapestry of a fulfilling life.

Embracing the Journey

Our journey began with the recognition of the power within you, the acknowledgment that you are a radiant being capable of creating a life filled with purpose and joy. Through daily affirmations, we explored the avenues of positive thinking, building a foundation for success, nurturing self-love and confidence, and cultivating gratitude. These affirmations were not mere words; they were the seeds planted in the garden of your mind, blossoming into a vibrant landscape of empowerment.

Navigating Change and Cultivating Resilience

In the chapter on embracing change and resilience, we danced through the rhythm of life's inevitable changes. Affirmations became the guiding stars, helping you navigate the seas of uncertainty with grace and courage. Together, we discovered the beauty of flexibility, resilience, and the unwavering trust that resides within you. Change, instead of being feared, became a canvas for self-discovery and triumph.

Mindfulness, Inner Peace, and the Power of Now

As we delved into mindfulness and inner peace, affirmations became the gentle whispers guiding you to the present moment. In the stillness of now, you found serenity, joy, and a profound sense of connection. Each affirmation was a step toward mindfulness, encouraging you to savor the richness of each experience, from the taste of a meal to the rhythm of your breath. Inner peace, the jewel of the soul, became a sanctuary you carried within, accessible in every moment.

Health and Well-being: A Symphony of Harmony

Health and well-being, the harmonious symphony of your existence, were explored through affirmations that celebrated your body, mind, and spirit. Affirmations became the pillars supporting your journey to vitality, positive thinking, mental clarity, emotional balance, and spiritual connection. You discovered that well-being is a holistic dance, where each element contributes to the vibrant tapestry of your life.

Evening Reflections and Gratitude: A Nightly Ritual of Grace

In the quiet moments of evening reflections and gratitude, you found solace and peace. Affirmations guided you to acknowledge the challenges, celebrate the victories, and express gratitude for the blessings of the day. The practice of reflection became a bridge to tranquility, preparing you for restful sleep and a promising tomorrow. Each evening, as you released the day with gratitude, you paved the way for a new dawn filled with endless possibilities.

A Promise for Tomorrow

And now, dear friend, as you close this book, remember that your journey doesn't end here; it's an ever-unfolding story of growth, wisdom, and joy. Affirmations are not just words on these pages; they are tools you carry with you, guiding your thoughts, shaping your actions, and fostering a positive mindset. Each affirmation is a reminder that you are the author of your life, and every day is an opportunity to write a chapter filled with love, purpose, and fulfillment.

Your Radiant Journey Continues

As you step into the next chapters of your life, may you carry the wisdom of these affirmations with you.

May you continue to dance with change, embrace the present moment, nurture your well-being, and find grace in the reflections of each evening. Your journey is a masterpiece in the making, and the affirmations you've embraced are the colors that paint the canvas of your existence.

A Heartfelt Thank You

Before we part ways, I extend a heartfelt thank you for allowing "Wisdom Whispers" to be a part of your journey. May its affirmations continue to echo in your heart, inspiring you to live a life guided by wisdom, love, and fulfillment. Remember, you are a radiant soul capable of creating a life that reflects the beauty within you.

Cheers to you, dear friend, and to the beautiful journey that lies ahead. May your days be filled with joy, your nights be restful, and your heart be a beacon of wisdom and love. Until we meet again on the pages of life, walk in the light of your own wisdom, and may each step be a dance of fulfillment.

Sample Affirmations for Various Life Areas

Self-Empowerment:

Affirmations for Self-Empowerment:

1. "I am the master of my fate and the captain of my soul. I have the power to shape my destiny with purpose and intention."

2. "Every challenge I face is an opportunity for growth and learning. I embrace difficulties as stepping stones to my success."

3. "My mind is a powerhouse of positivity. I banish self-doubt and embrace the limitless potential within me."

4. "I trust in my abilities and believe in my unique gifts. I am a beacon of confidence, radiating strength to overcome any obstacle."

5. "I am not defined by my past. I release any lingering doubts and boldly step into a future of endless possibilities."

6. "I am resilient, adaptable, and capable of overcoming any adversity. I am stronger than I think, and I face challenges with courage."

7. "My thoughts create my reality, and I choose thoughts that empower and uplift me. I am the architect of my own happiness."

Repeat these affirmations regularly to reinforce a positive and empowering mindset. Customize them to align with your personal goals and aspirations.

Relationships:

Affirmations for nurturing positive relationships:

1. "I attract and cultivate loving, supportive relationships into my life. My connections are built on trust, respect, and understanding."

2. "I communicate openly and authentically, fostering deep connections with those around me. My words promote love, empathy, and harmony."

3. "Every relationship in my life adds value and contributes to my personal growth. I am surrounded by positive influences and genuine connections."

4. "I am worthy of love and belonging. I embrace vulnerability, allowing meaningful connections to flourish in my life."

5. "I release any negative energy from past relationships. My heart is open to new connections that align with my values and aspirations."

6. "I am a source of positivity in my relationships. I offer support, encouragement, and kindness to those I love."

7. "I am grateful for the love and companionship in my life. My relationships are a source of joy, fulfillment, and mutual respect."

Use these affirmations to reinforce a positive mindset and contribute to the health and growth of your relationships. Feel free to customize them to resonate with your unique experiences and intentions.

Professional Success:

Affirmations for fostering professional success:

1. "I am confident in my abilities and attract success into every aspect of my professional life. I am destined for greatness."

2. "Every challenge is an opportunity for growth and advancement. I embrace challenges with a positive mindset, knowing they lead to success."

3. "I am a skilled and capable professional. My expertise is valued, and I contribute meaningfully to the success of my team and organization."

4. "My career path is filled with abundance, prosperity, and opportunities for advancement. I am on the journey to fulfilling my professional aspirations."

5. "I am open to learning and adapting to new opportunities. I embrace change as a catalyst for growth and improvement in my career."

6. "I radiate confidence in my professional endeavors. I am a magnet for positive opportunities, recognition, and career advancement."

7. "I set clear goals for my professional success and take consistent, purposeful actions to achieve them. I am creating the career of my dreams."

Repeat these affirmations regularly to reinforce a positive mindset and enhance your focus on professional success. Customize them to align with your specific career goals and aspirations.

Health and Wellness:

Affirmations for promoting health and wellness:

1. "My body is a temple, and I treat it with love and respect. I am grateful for the gift of health and vitality."

2. "I make choices that nourish and support my well-being. Every action I take contributes to my overall health."

3. "I am in tune with my body's needs, and I listen to its signals. I honor my body with balanced nutrition and mindful movement."

4. "Every breath I take fills me with energy and vitality. I am alive, vibrant, and radiating good health."

5. "I release stress from my mind and body. Each moment of relaxation contributes to my overall well-being."

6. "I am the master of my habits, and I choose habits that promote a healthy and fulfilling life. I am creating a foundation for long-lasting wellness."

7. "I am resilient, and my body has the innate ability to heal. I trust in the healing power within me and take actions that support my well-being."

Incorporate these affirmations into your daily routine to promote a positive mindset and support your journey toward health and wellness. Feel free to personalize them to better resonate with your specific wellness goals.

Overcoming Limiting Beliefs:

Affirmations designed to help overcome limiting beliefs:

1. "I release all self-doubt and embrace the boundless potential within me. I am capable of achieving greatness."

2. "My mind is free from the shackles of limiting beliefs. I trust in my abilities and believe in my unique strengths."

3. "I let go of the fear of failure. Mistakes are stepping stones on my path to success, and each one propels me forward."

4. "I am worthy of success, love, and abundance. My past does not define my future, and I am open to new possibilities."

5. "I replace negative thoughts with positive affirmations. I am the architect of my thoughts, shaping a mindset of confidence and self-assurance."

6. "I challenge and overcome my limiting beliefs with courage and resilience. I am rewriting my story with positivity and empowerment."

7. "I trust in my journey. Every obstacle is an opportunity, and I approach challenges with a mindset of curiosity and growth."

Repeat these affirmations regularly to reprogram your mindset and overcome any limiting beliefs that may be holding you back. Adjust them to resonate with your personal experiences and aspirations.

Mindfulness and Presence:

Affirmations to cultivate mindfulness and presence:

1. "I am fully present in each moment, savoring the richness of life unfolding around me."

2. "My mind is clear, and I approach each day with mindful awareness and intention."

3. "I release worries about the past and future, finding peace and joy in the present moment."

4. "Each breath I take grounds me in the here and now, fostering a deep sense of calm and serenity."

5. "I embrace silence and stillness, allowing space for mindfulness to blossom in my daily life."

6. "I let go of distractions and focus my attention on the beauty and grace present in every moment."

7. "Mindfulness is a gift I give myself daily. I am attuned to the present, finding joy in the simple pleasures of life."

Incorporate these affirmations into your mindfulness practice to enhance your ability to stay present and fully engage with the experiences of each moment. Feel free to adapt them to align with your personal journey toward mindfulness and presence.

Gratitude and Positivity:

Affirmations to foster gratitude and positivity:

1. "I am grateful for the abundance in my life, both big and small. My heart is open to receiving and acknowledging the blessings around me."

2. "Positivity is my default state of mind. I attract joy and positivity into every aspect of my life."

3. "I appreciate the beauty in every moment, finding gratitude in the simple pleasures of life."

4. "I am a magnet for positive energy. I radiate positivity and attract uplifting experiences into my life."

5. "I choose to focus on what is good and positive in my life. My thoughts shape my reality, and I choose to see the bright side."

6. "Gratitude is the key to my happiness. I express gratitude freely and cultivate a mindset of abundance."

7. "I find joy in the journey, and my heart is filled with gratitude for the lessons and experiences that contribute to my personal growth."

Incorporate these affirmations into your daily routine to cultivate a mindset of gratitude and positivity. Adjust them to resonate with your personal experiences and enhance your focus on the positive aspects of life.

Journal Prompts for Reflection and Goal Setting

Reflection Journal Prompts:

1. **Current State of Mind:**
- How do you feel right now, both emotionally and mentally?
- Are there any specific thoughts or concerns occupying your mind?

2. **Gratitude Journaling:**
- List three things you're grateful for today.
- How did these things positively impact your day?

3. **Accomplishments and Achievements:**
- Reflect on recent accomplishments, no matter how small.
- What strengths or skills did you showcase during these achievements?

4. **Challenges and Growth:**
- Describe a recent challenge you faced.
- What did you learn from overcoming this challenge, and how did you grow?

5. **Joyful Moments:**

- Recall a moment that brought you joy recently.
- What about that moment made you feel happy, and how can you replicate or create more of those moments?

6. **Self-Reflection on Relationships:**

- How have your relationships influenced your mood and well-being lately?
- Is there a relationship that requires attention or improvement?

7. **Mindfulness Check-in:**

- Reflect on a moment when you were fully present.
- What practices or activities help you stay mindful, and how can you incorporate more of them into your routine?

Goal Setting Journal Prompts:

1. **Overall Life Vision:**

- Envision your ideal life. What does it look like in terms of career, relationships, health, and personal development?

2. **S.M.A.R.T. Goals:**

- Define one specific, measurable, achievable, relevant, and time-bound goal for the next month.
- Break it down into smaller tasks and create a timeline.

3. Personal Development:

- What skills or knowledge do you want to acquire or improve upon in the next six months?
- How will these enhancements contribute to your overall growth?

4. Health and Wellness:

- Set a health-related goal, whether it's related to nutrition, exercise, or mental well-being.
- What actionable steps can you take to achieve this goal.

5. Career Aspirations:

- Where do you see yourself in your career one year from now?
- Identify a specific career-related goal and outline the steps to achieve it.

6. Relationship Goals:

- Reflect on your key relationships. What are your goals for nurturing and improving them?

- How can you express love and appreciation to those important to you?

7. **Joy and Hobbies:**

- Identify a hobby or activity that brings you joy.
- Set a goal to engage in this activity regularly and explore how it positively impacts your overall well-being.

"In the dance of life, let the music be your own wisdom, the steps guided by love, and the rhythm a heartbeat of gratitude. As you close this chapter, remember: You are the author of a radiant story, and every day is a chance to write a symphony of fulfillment. Embrace the melody of your existence, dance with joy in your heart, and let the echoes of wisdom whispers guide you toward a life abundantly lived."

Milton Keynes UK
Ingram Content Group UK Ltd.
UKHW020237301123
433483UK00016B/823